1 MONTH OF FREE READING

at

www.ForgottenBooks.com

By purchasing this book you are eligible for one month membership to ForgottenBooks.com, giving you unlimited access to our entire collection of over 700,000 titles via our web site and mobile apps.

To claim your free month visit:

www.forgottenbooks.com/free611902

ISBN 978-0-484-73777-7
PIBN 10611902

Ewart, John Skirving

THE KINGDOM PAPERS, No. 6.

A CANADIAN NAVY

iese papers (including the back numbers) will be sent, free of charge, to all applicants.

JOHN S. EWART,
Ottawa, Ont.

A CANADIAN NAVY.

(In order to draw attention to the purpose for which quotations are employed, italics not appearing in the original are sometimes made use of.)

ON two questions Canada appears not to have arrived at very certain conclusions: Does she want a navy of any sort? And, if so, what sort of a navy ought it to be?

Indecision must be attributed to two main causes: First, the indefinite character of our political relationship with the United Kingdom; and secondly, unfamiliarity with the history of the subject. In the present Paper, I shall endeavor to supply material for the formation of judgment, rather than to advocate the adoption of my own views.

Our Obligations.

In previous Papers I have endeavored to define the nature of the relationship which exists between Canada and the United Kingdom, but I am not sure that I have been able to do more than make clear the peculiar anomalies of its character. Nominally, legally, and, very largely, internationally, Canada is still part of the British Empire—is still one of those countries governed legislatively by the British parliament, and, administratively, by the Colonial Office. As a matter of fact, Canada is almost completely an independent state; and everyone agrees that domination from London is, for the future, as impossible as from St. Petersburg. Every step from colony to kingdom has been contested—our right to legislate as we pleased; our right to administer our affairs as we pleased; our right to negotiate our trade and boundary treaties as we pleased. But all these contests belong to history. Nothing of them remains. With respect to all of them we are really, although not yet nominally, in the position of an independent state.

The contradiction between the real and the merely legal has led, quite naturally, to opposite opinion as to the position of Canada

A CANADIAN NAVY.

(In order to draw attention to the purpose for which quotations are employed, italics not appearing in the original are sometimes made use of.)

ON two questions Canada appears not to have arrived at very certain conclusions: Does she want a navy of any sort? And, if so, what sort of a navy ought it to be?

Indecision must be attributed to two main causes: First, the indefinite character of our political relationship with the United Kingdom; and secondly, unfamiliarity with the history of the subject. In the present Paper, I shall endeavor to supply material for the formation of judgment, rather than to advocate the adoption of my own views.

Our Obligations.

In previous Papers I have endeavored to define the nature of the relationship which exists between Canada and the United Kingdom, but I am not sure that I have been able to do more than make clear the peculiar anomalies of its character. Nominally, legally, and, very largely, internationally, Canada is still part of the British Empire—is still one of those countries governed legislatively by the British parliament, and, administratively, by the Colonial Office. As a matter of fact, Canada is almost completely an independent state; and everyone agrees that domination from London is, for the future, as impossible as from St. Petersburg. Every step from colony to kingdom has been contested—our right to legislate as we pleased; our right to administer our affairs as we pleased; our right to negotiate our trade and boundary treaties as we pleased. But all these contests belong to history. Nothing of them remains. With respect to all of them we are really, although not yet nominally, in the position of an independent state.

The contradiction between the real and the merely legal has led, quite naturally, to opposite opinion as to the position of Canada.

in the event of the United Kingdom being engaged in war. If we are part of the British Empire, then, most certainly, when the Empire is at war, we are belligerent—for the whole includes the less. And if, on the other hand, we are an independent state, then we are at war only when we wish. But the fact is, that we are neither part of the Empire nor independent—or rather, nominally, we are the one, and really, we are the other.

From one point of view, there is no answer to what Sir Frederick Pollock has said:—

"The law of nations knows nothing of an international unit, whatever its internal constitution may be, making war and peace in sections. Austria cannot be at peace while Hungary is at war; and if the United States go to war, Massachusetts or California cannot be neutral. . . . . And what would Sir Wilfrid Laurier say to a claim of the Province of Quebec to have no part in the wars of the Dominion" (a).

But Sir Frederick begs the question, which is not whether a unit is divisible (about which we may assume general agreement), but whether it is a unit that we are speaking about. Nominally it is, but really it is not. What does the law of nations know about a case of that sort? Nothing? Very well, the law of nations cannot settle it. There are very many other points upon which there is no law of nations.

From the other point of view—that Canada is an independent state related to the United Kingdom only by allegiance to the common sovereign—the position is likewise clear. When England and Scotland were separate kingdoms under the same king, one might be, and indeed was, at war without the co-operation of the other. And when the British parliament was arranging for the union of the crowns of England and Hanover, one section of the statute provided:

"That in case the crown and imperial dignity of this realm shall hereafter come to any person, not being a native of the Kingdom of England, this nation be not obliged to engage in any war for the defence of any dominions or territories which do not belong to the Crown of England, without the consent of parliament" (b).

Canadians may be pardoned if in their anomalous political situation they take the view of their position more favorable to themselves; and, when the history of the relation between the two countries is remembered, it cannot be thought extraordinary that

(a) *Times*, July, 1911.
(b) 12, 13 William III, cap. 2.

the British authorities should be found assenting to that view. Canada has most clearly and authoritatively asserted her freedom of action in case of a British war. She has done so principally in three ways:

(1) By the specific declaration of her Prime Minister speaking as such from his place in the House of Commons (a).

(2) By the specific communication of that declaration to the British authorities at the Imperial Conferences of 1902 and 1911 (b).

(3) By the clause of the statute providing for the construction of our navy, which requires that parliament shall be summoned in order to determine what shall be done with our ships in case of war.

And the British authorities have just as clearly assented to the validity of the Canadian claim. They have done so in the following ways:

(1) By leaving unchallenged the answer of Canada and Australia to the request of the Colonial Defence Committee, at the Colonial Conference of 1902, for

"Some assurance as to the strength of the contingents which they should be able to place at the disposal of His Majesty's government for extra-colonial service in a war with a European power."

The answer was that the matter would be considered "when the need arose"; and to this Mr. Chamberlain made no suggestion of legal or constitutional obligation.

(2) At a sub-conference "on the naval and military defence of the Empire" 1909, the main point agreed to was

"That each part of the Empire is willing to make its preparations on such lines as will enable it, *should it so desire*, to take its share in the general defence of the Empire" (c).

(3) In his reporting to the House of Commons the result of the sub-conference, Mr. Asquith said:

"The result is a plan for so organizing the forces of the Crown wherever they are, that while preserving the complete autonomy of each Dominion, *should the Dominions desire to assist in the defence of the Empire in a real emergency*, their forces could be rapidly combined into one homogeneous imperial army" (d).

There was not, at this sub-conference, the slightest suggestion of legal or constitutional obligation on the part of the Dominions.

(a) Ante, p. 110.
(b) Ante, p. 110.
(c) Cd. 4948, p. 19. See also p. 38.
(d) Ibid. p. 19.

(4) At the Imperial Conference of 1911, it was agreed and declared that:

"The naval services and forces of the Dominions of Canada and Australia will be *exclusively* under the control of their respective governments" (a).

If further evidence upon this point be necessary, reference may be made to the valuable work *Responsible Government in the Dominions*, written by Mr. A. B. Keith of the Colonial Office, in which, when discussing the right of a Governor-General to place colonial troops under a British officer he said (p. 198) that such

"doctrine would involve the theory that the imperial government could insist on colonial forces taking part in a war, a doctrine opposed to the fundamental principles of self-government, which *leaves to a colony to decide how far it will participate in wars due to imperial policy.*"

It is perfectly clear therefore: (1) That Canada has officially asserted her freedom of action in case of a British war, and (2) that the United Kingdom has assented to the constitutional validity of the claim.

Uncertainty Nevertheless: But the absence of constitutional obligation to take part in British wars does not relieve us from uncertainties, of two kinds, attributable to our anomalous relationship with the United Kingdom. First, the general and popular view of our obligation is the precise contrary of that which I have indicated, and it is extremely unlikely that under the foolish excitements of declared war, the voice of reason will have any chance of being heard. We are free; but many of us believe that we are bound by moral as well as constitutional ties, no matter what the character of the war, and we shall probably act accordingly. Secondly, although we may wish to be non-combatant, the enemy of Britain may (as she would have a perfect right to do) treat us as belligerent, and, by attacking, force us into hostilities (b).

The effect, then, of our anomalous relationship with the United Kingdom is that we may at any moment be involved in a war in which we have no direct interest; and although we have, in one view, a perfectly legal and constitutional as well as moral right (c) to remain non-combatant, in another view, it is very doubtful whether we should ever be able to do it.

(a) Cd. 5746–2, p. I.
(b) Cf. ante, p. 78.
(c) Material for opinion as to our obligation from a moral point of view may be found, ante, pp. 32–48.

Our Needs.

We have considered the situation from the point of view of our obligations and have found that, although we have none, we may get into plenty of trouble because of them (Our case is as anomalous as that). Let us look at the subject from the point of view of our needs—our needs unencumbered by these unreal obligations. For we must remember that if we are under no obligation to assist the United Kingdom in case of war, she, on the other hand, is under no obligation to assist us. Under those circumstances, what are our needs?

The answer to the question is not I think difficult, for very clearly, a navy would be of little service to us in case of war with the United States (the fighting would be on land); and, very fortunately, we have no other neighbors to quarrel with. It is in the last degree improbable that we should find ground for war-contest with trans-Atlantic or trans-Pacific nations. Past wars have been due to religious, dynastic or territorial quarrels. With far-off nations we shall never be at issue upon any of these grounds, and we need have no apprehension of an unprovoked war of mere conquest.

Why do I say so? Because of the Monroe Doctrine? Are we mean enough to shelter ourselves under Yankee bluster? Patience a moment and let me explain. The Monroe doctrine has a wrong name. It should be called the Canning policy, for to that great Englishman—George Canning— are we indebted for one of the most beneficial of all principles regulative of international relations. Observe its origin. The Spanish colonies in America were in revolt; Spain, herself enfeebled by French aggression, was powerless to enforce obedience; and the Holy Alliance (with France as chief executioner) was preparing a partition of American territories among its members. To the United Kingdom the prospect was full of menace and danger. Not long ago she had lost the best of her American possessions, and she viewed with consternation the threatened aggrandisement of all her rivals. Unaided, she was powerless to oppose the designs of France, Russia, Austria and Prussia, and it was with the greatest difficulty, and only after the most persistent effort that Canning was able to persuade Monroe to send to Congress his famous message (23 December, 1823). It had the desired effect. The United Kingdom was safe.

But for the Canning policy, what would have been to-day the situation in this hemisphere? Do you imagine that Mexico would be without naval protection? that Costa Rica would be without an army—that, indeed, by this time, there would have been a Costa

(4) At the Imperial Conference of 1911 t was agreed and declared that:

"The naval services and forces of the Dominio of Canada and Australia will be *exclusively* under the control of their respecti governments" (a).

If further evidence upon this point be ne ssary, reference may be made to the valuable work *Responsible overnment in the Dominions*, written by Mr. A. B. Keith of the Conial Office, in which, when discussing the right of a Governor-G ral to place colonial troops under a British officer he said (p. 1! that such

"doctrine would involve the theory that the imper government could insist on colonial forces taking part in a war, a doctrine ed to the *fundamental principles of self-government, which leaves to a colo t decide how far it will participate in wars due to imperial policy.*"

It is perfectly clear therefore: (1) Th Canada has officially asserted her freedom of action in case of a 1 ish war, and (2) that the United Kingdom has assented to the c stitutional validity of the claim.

Uncertainty Nevertheless: But the ab ce of constitutional obligation to take part in British wai d s not relieve us from uncertainties, of two kinds, attribu le to our anomalous relationship with the United Kingdom. rs the general and popular view of our obligation is the cise contrary of that which I have indicated, and it is extren y unlikely that under the foolish excitements of declared wai the voice of reason will have any chance of being heard. W are free; but many of us believe that we are bound by moral well as constitutional ties, no matter what the character of the wi an 1 we shall probably act accordingly. Secondly, although we nas wish to be non-combatant, the enemy of Britain may (as would have a perfect right to do) treat us as belligerent, and, by attacking, force us into hostilities (b).

The effect, then, of our anomalous relationship with the United Kingdom is that we may at any moment involved in a which we have no direct interest; and although we h view, a perfectly legal and constitutional a well to remain non-combatant, in another vic , whether we should ever be able to do it.

(a) Cd. 5746-2, p. I.
(b) Cf. ante, p. 78.
(c) Material for opinion as to our obligation from ante, pp. 32–48.

We have consid ed the situation from the point of view of our obligations and hav found that, although we have none, we may get into plenty of tr ble because of them (Our case is as anomalous as that). Let us lo at the subject from the point of view of our needs—our needs u ncumbered by these unreal obligations. For we must rememl er at if we are under no obligation to assist the United Kingdom in se of war, she, on the other hand, is under no obligation to assist s. Under those circumstances, what are our needs?

The answer to ie question is not I think difficult, for very clearly, a navy woulc e of little service to us in case of war with the United States (the fi ting would be on land); and, very fortunately, we have no other n hbors to quarrel with. It is in the last degree improbable that we iould find ground for war-contest with trans-Atlantic or trans-P ific nations. Past wars have been due to religious, dynastic o territorial quarrels. With far-off nations we shall never be at issu upon any of these grounds, and we need have no apprehension of unprovoked war of mere conquest.

Why do I say ? Because of the Monroe Doctrine? Are we mean enough to clter ourselves under Yankee bluster? Patience a moment and t me explain. The Monroe doctrine has a wrong name. It sh ld be called the Canning policy, for, to that great Englishman orge Canning— are we indebted for one of the most beneficial o all principles regulative of international relations. Observe its gin. The Spanish colonies in America were in revolt; Spain, hrself enfeebled by French aggression, we powerless to enforce edience; and the Holy Alliance (with Fr — jal as chief executioner wa preparing a partition of Americ , to tories among its members. To the United Kingdom t' e fre- was full of me d danger. Not long ago she h Jnited of her Ame ssions, and she viewed ent that the threatened mont of all her riv

is of Fr

greatest

Canning it so desire, to

mous m

e situation is, I nall we not under

Rica? and that Canada could devote almost her whole revenue to material development? George Canning's achievement has far outrun his conception or intention. For his own country's safety he prevented the aggrandisement. That was his sole purpose. But the effect of his act has been to separate the Americas from European conflagrations. Those who know their earlier history can alone appreciate the value of Canning's service to the peoples of this hemisphere, Mexico, Costa Rica, &c. To the oft-repeated assertion that we ought not to depend upon the United States, the proper reply is that Canning saw no humiliation in community of interests with the United States or in co-operation in support of them.

But is it not possible that some nation may flout the Canning policy, and attempt the occupation of Canada? No. No nation has the strength, and no nation is sufficiently foolish to make the attempt. Canada will never have to appeal to the Canning policy. The fact that it has existed, and has been accepted and acted upon for nearly ninety years, and the fact that not only the United Kingdom and the United States are as much or more interested than ever in maintaining it, but that the whole hemisphere is now fairly well occupied by nations who would enthusiastically combine in upholding it—these facts make attack with a view to occupation impossible. The Canning policy is not our defence; it is our guarantee that defence shall not be necessary.

The suggestion has been made that Germany is seeking territorial expansion, and that if she could only dissipate the British fleet, she might turn Canada into an Alsace-Lorraine. Germans are not lunatics. If they shall ever be in a position to occupy any part of the King's dominions, they will go to Africa or India. They will not add the nations of America to the list of their European enemies. They will pursue the line of least resistance. Surrounded by armed nations, Germany will never attempt the subjection of any part of the Americas. If she did, what do you imagine would be happening in Europe? If the British fleet is our sole protection against German occupation, what is it that protects the Argentine Republic?

When I say that, apart from her association with the United Kingdom, Canada is in no danger of over-sea attack, I do not mean, of course, that such attack is beyond the bounds of possibility. Huxley once said that a crocodile with a tail a hundred miles long was not an impossibility. All that I do say, is that the chances of it are remote; that its possibility belongs to a world-situation entirely different from the one in which we live; and that for these reasons it would be foolish to make extensive arrangements for war, or to provide for conditions the character of which we are quite unable to foresee or forecast. Our expenditure ought to be governed by the probable and the natural, and not by the unlikely possible.

Summary.

The following propositions result from what has been said:

(1) The political relations between Canada and the United Kingdom are anomalous. Theoretically Canada is a part of the British Empire. Really she is not.

(2) Canada is under no legal, constitutional, or moral obligation to assist the United Kingdom in case of war.

(3) Nevertheless Canada may be involved in British wars in which she has no direct interest:

(a) By her own choice, influenced by the existence of the anomaly, or

(b) At the discretion of the enemy.

(4) Apart from our association with the United Kingdom, we are not in need of a navy.

(a) It would be of no practical service against the United States.

(b) We are in no danger of over-sea attack.

What Ought to be Done?

Readers who agree with what has been said will see that our proper course of action is very clear. If it be true that our embarrassment is due solely to the anomalous character of our political relationship with the United Kingdom, undoubtedly we ought to seek relief by removing the anomaly. At present, as I have frequently pointed out, we have no arrangement with the United Kingdom for co-operation in case of war. The only agreement that we have is that each of the Associated Kingdoms will

"make its preparations on such lines as will enable it, *should it so desire*, to take its share in the general defence . . . ." (a)

But every kingdom is free to do as it pleases. The situation is, I repeat, both foolish and dangerous. Shall we or shall we not under

(a) Ante, p. 147.

all circumstances, take up the quarrel of any one of us? Why not settle the question?

The anomalous ought to be ended. Our nationhood must not only be real, but must be acknowledged. Our political situation and relationship must be clear. And when we undertsand it, we shall consider more carefully, if less anxiously, our attitude towards world-affairs. We shall probably endeavor to enter into some reasonable agreement with the others of His Majesty's dominions, and our naval policy will be appropriate to our obligations.

Some of my readers will not accept my presentation of our obligations and our needs, and they will have little patience with my analysis. They will refuse to discuss legal and constitutional points. They would strike the words *"should it so desire"* out of the resolution of the conference. They would cheerfully pledge themselves to join in any war in which the United Kingdom might ever be engaged. And if you were to ask them if they would fight not merely for the United Kingdom but for Japan, if the United Kingdom had to implement her treaty with that country, they would answer with an emphatic affirmative.

But they should remember that in Canada there are very many people who do not share their enthusiasm. They must be aware that a large majority of Canadians would not agree to strike out the words "should it so desire"—would refuse to give an absolutely unconditional and unqualified guarantee of assistance, and they, therefore, must agree that the only rational course is to discuss the matter with our associates, and to endeavor to arrive at some satisfactory conclusion.

Although the course of action just suggested (the removal of the anomaly and the uncertainty) is unquestionably both proper and reasonable, perhaps we may quite safely assume that it will not be adopted. Our nationalism, although real, is too recent for acceptance in all its logical results. After the war of American independence, and the treaty-acknowledgment of that independence, the United Kingdom was unable for a time to think of the Americans as other than colonials, or to treat them as forming a sovereign nation. Very many people do not as yet recognise the fact that we have sole control over our actions, and that if the United Kingdom wishes to count upon our war-assistance she must come to some agreement about it. Probably, therefore, no attempt at agreement will be made. Probably the anomalies and uncertainties of the present situation will for some time continue.

Do We Want a Navy?

Meanwhile, then, what ought we to do? Some of our people object to the construction of a navy. They urge that the only wars in which we shall be interested will be British wars— wars in which Canada will have no direct interest; that we are under no obligation to assist in such wars; that if we do take part in them, we can do so more effectively (as in the Boer and other wars) by sending our men, than by contributing ships to the already all-powerful British navy; that in such wars the obligation to protect the trade routes would rest upon the United Kingdom; and that whether or not that obligation is acknowledged, her necessities would compel her to protect wheat ships, whether they sailed from Canada or Argentina.

Other Canadians argue otherwise. Occasionally they base themselves upon legal obligation. More frequently they declare that Canada's safety depends entirely upon the British navy. And not seldom, do they decline all discussion, contenting themselves with references to the Union Jack.

I have already indicated my views upon the debatable points in issue between these two classes of Canadians. My opinion upon them is altogether with the no-navy men. But while accepting their arguments, there is a further point to be considered before we can agree with their conclusion.

Consider the following: When negotiating the recent Declaration of London, the United Kingdom endeavored to obtain general prohibition of the practice of conversion of merchant-vessels into war-ships (except at a port of the proprietor nation). She was unsuccessful, and the actual situation is that immediately upon the out-break of war, fast commercial vessels may come into action in all parts of the world. While the supremacy of the British navy lasts, no foreign war-ships will block the trade routes, but raiders and commerce-destroyers may pursue their guerilla depredations indefinitely.

Let me dwell a little upon this point, for it was the main factor in the conversion of Australia and the British Admiralty from the idea of colonial contributions to the British navy, and of their adoption of the Canadian idea of separate navies.

Mr. Chamberlain (in this, as in his other schemes, opposed to colonial enfranchisement) pressed for contributions, and at the Colonial Conference of 1902, presented a document issued by the Admiralty entitled: ''Memorandum on Sea-power and the

Principles involved in it" (a). From it I quote the following extra-ordinary paragraphs:

"In the foregoing remarks the word *defence* does not appear. It is omitted advisedly because the primary object of the British navy is not to defend anything, but to attack the fleets of the enemy, and, by defeating them, to afford protection to British Dominions, shipping and commerce. This is the ultimate aim. To use the word *defence* would be misleading, because the word carries with it the idea of a thing to be defended, which would divert attention to local defence, instead of fixing it on the force from which attack is to be expected."

In support of this view, the First Lord of the Admiralty (Lord Selborne) appeared at a meeting of the Conference, and said that

"The real problem which this Empire has to face in the case of a naval war is simply and absolutely to find out where the ships of the enemy are, to concentrate the greatest possible force where those ships are, and to destroy those ships. . . . It follows from this that there can be no localisation of naval forces in the strict sense of the word. . . . I want to see from all parts of the Empire a personal contribution to the navy. . . ." (b).

That doctrine might be good enough to apply to the colonies, but for its application to British coasts, let me refer readers to the handbook of the Navy League for the same year as the Conference (1902):

"There should always be an effective reserve squadron, *absolutely confined to home waters*, sufficient to hold the channel and protect the coasts and commerce of the United Kingdom, *in addition to the coast defence ships* which would be required for active local defence."

The Editor added:

"The experience of the Spanish-American war has shown that public opinion will always clamor for a home squadron. We had a squadron in the channel all through the Trafalgar campaign."

Nelson went into the Mediterranean and over to the West Indies "to find out where the ships of the enemy" were, but the channel fleet never left British shores, for fear that the ships of the enemy might after all be in the North Sea and not in the Carribean.

Nevertheless, Mr. Chamberlain had some success at the Conference. Colonial contributions were increased, but colonial feeling was rising, and in the following year Senator Matheson of Australia in a notable address at the Royal Colonial Institute, vigorously attacked

(a) Cd. 1299, p. 54; and see Cd. 1597.
(b) Proceedings, p. 15.

the Selborne idea. He quoted as against the First Lord, the opinion of Sir George Clarke:

"Small expeditions directed, not to effect territorial conquests, but to destroy national resources, may nevertheless, as in the past, evade a superior navy. Such expeditions are of the nature of raids."

The truth of this statement is, of course, perfectly obvious, and at the next meeting of the Colonial Conference (1907), it was accepted as a basis for the reconsideration of the contribution method of defence. The new First Lord (Tweedmouth) said:

"In the opinion of the government, while the distribution of the fleet must be determined by strategical requirements of which the Admiralty are to judge, it would be of great assistance if the Colonial Governments would undertake to provide for local service in the imperial squadrons, the smaller vessels that are *useful for defence against possible raids* or for co-operation with a squadron; and also to equip and maintain docks and fitting establishments which can be used by His Majesty's ships. It will further be of much assistance, if coaling facilities are provided, and arrangements can be made for a supply of coal and naval stores which otherwise would have to be sent out specially or purchased locally.

"I understand that in Australia, it is desired to start some naval service of your own. Perhaps I might suggest that if the provision of the smaller craft which are necessarily incident to the work of a great fleet of modern battleships could be made locally, *it would be a very great help to the general work of the navy.* You cannot take the small craft, such as torpedo boats and submarines, across the ocean; and for warships to arrive in South Africa, or in Australia, or in New Zealand, or in Canada, and find ready to their hand well trained men in good vessels of this kind, would be an enormous advantage to them. It would be an enormous advantage to find ready to hand, men well trained, ready to take a part in the work of the fleet. There is, I think, the further advantage in these small flotillas, that they will be *an admirable means of coast defence; that you will be able by the use of them to avoid practically all danger from any sudden raid which might be made by a cruising squadron (a).*"

In Mr. Deakin's speech may be found the following:

"The Committee of Imperial Defence, after giving this question full consideration, have decided that *a regular attacking force is not to be anticipated in our Antipodean situation under any circumstances that it is necessary to directly provide for in advance. They look forward to the possibilities of a raid, consisting in all likelihood of some four fast half-armored or partly armored cruisers,* carrying forces of from five hundred to, at the outside, one thousand men. Even an expedition of those small dimensions, calling for a very considerable provision in the way of fuel and other arrangements, would make only a transitory dash for our ports and our shipping, rather than a series of prolonged attacks. But whatever the nature of the assault is to be, its possibility leaves the large population of our sea-bound states with a sense of insecurity, emphasised

(a) Proceedings, pp. 130, 1.

by the probability of the withdrawal of the squadron some thousands of miles away to deal with the expected enemy there. Consequently the demand for some harbor and coast defence has been pressed upon the minds of the people in general, and has been lately several times considered in parliament. *It is thought that while it may be the best possible naval strategy to withdraw the squadron to remote portions of the seas surrounding Australia, the contingency of our being raided, even by a few cruisers, and of our commerce being driven into the harbors or destroyed or enclosed in the harbors, is not one that a community ought to contemplate unmoved"* (a).

I have quoted enough for proof of the point that I am endeavoring to make. I now turn to those Canadians who oppose the creation of a navy, and I submit to them whether, notwithstanding their arguments (with which I agree) some defence against sea-raiders is not necessary. We have no control over the making of war. We may be in it, and the enemies' depradators may be at work next week. Ought we, or ought we not, to provide for such an eventuality (b)?

Contribution or Construction.

What has just been said has close relation to the question whether we ought to make contributions to the British navy or to undertake for ourselves the construction of war-vessels. But as that question cannot be adequately argued in the absence of considerations supplied by the history of the subject, let me give a short sketch of it.

Australia has always been anxious about the ownership of the islands which cloud her northerly and easterly coasts. Had she had her way, they would all be British. Now they belong to everybody—the ownership of one of them, New Guinea (almost within gunshot of Australia) is divided between Australia, Germany and Holland; and the sovereignty of the New Hebrides group is shared with France. Australia has, therefore, some reason for her anxiety about naval protection, and none the less because her own huge, unoccupied areas may tempt the rapacity of nations needing space. The insecurity of her position forms a strong contrast to the safety of the Canadian situation.

(a) Proceedings, p. 474.

(b) Since writing the above, the following telegram from Australia has appeared in the newspapers:—"Grave concern is felt throughout the Commonwealth over the assertion that all overseas vessels subsidized by foreign countries are easily convertible into commerce destroyers in war time. Private advices received in this country state liners flying the German flag are especially equipped for this contingency. As a result of this feeling of apprehension a resolution has been moved in the Federal parliament to the effect that action be taken forthwith to discourage such shipping from trading in Australian waters. Premier Fisher said: 'We say most emphatically that ships of other nations which come to trade in our waters must not presume too much on our good nature and equip themselves so that they may act as ships of war upon the declaration of hostilities'—words which were greeted with ringing cheers. The resolution was finally withdrawn."

As early as 1882, Australian defence was considered by a royal commission under the presidency of Lord Carnavon (a); and in 1886, Admiral Tryon carried on negotiations with the governments of the Australasian colonies with a view to the increase of the Australian squadron at joint expense. No agreement was arrived at, and the subject was relegated to the Colonial Conference of 1887.

That Conference was held primarily for the purpose of considering the question of defence; and with a view of putting the colonial premiers in proper frame of mind, the British Prime Minister remarked at the opening meeting that:

"The English colonies comprise some of the finest and most desirable portions of the earth's surface. The desire for foreign and colonial possessions is increasing among the nations of Europe" (b).

Actuated by such considerations, Australia entered into an agreement with the British Government by which five cruisers and two torpedo gunboats were to be added to the Australian squadron; that these vessels should be retained "within the limits of the Australian station"; that they should be removed only "with the consent of the colonial Government"; and that, of the cost involved, the colonies should pay not more than £126,000 per annum. This was the commencement of what has been called colonial contributions to the British navy. It was an agreement for defence by so many ships for so much money. The ships were provided and the money was paid. Canada had no anxieties about her defence. She made no complaint of exposure to attack. And having no agreement for protection she paid nothing for it.

At the conference of 1897, Mr. Chamberlain pressed for further contributions to the British navy. He got £30,000 per annum from Cape Colony, and a continuation of the Australasian agreement. To Canada he addressed the following argument:—

"Now let it not be supposed for a moment that I suggest as probable—I hardly like to think that it is even possible—that there should be a war between Canada, or on behalf of Canada, either with the United States of America, or with any of the other powers with which she may come into contact; but, what I do say is this, that if Canada had not behind her to-day, and does not continue to have behind her this great military and naval power of Great Britain, she would have to make concessions to her neighbors, and to accept views which might be extremely distasteful to her, in order to remain permanently on good terms with them. She would not be able to, it would be impossible that she should, herself control all the details of her own destiny; she would be to a greater or less extent, in spite of the bravery of her population and the patriotism of her people, she would still be, to a great extent, a dependent country" (c).

(a) Col. Confer. of 1887, p. 295.
(b) Proceedings, p. 6.
(c) Ibid, p. 8.

There is a certain amount of validity in that argument, and it might (if we felt sufficiently impressed by it) be a reason for adding enormously to our land forces, although clearly, not for contributing to the British navy. But we are not sufficiently impressed— partly, perhaps, because we have been taught by British policy that we must expect to have to accept views that are quite distasteful to us, and partly because such views are not likely to be very fateful. Mr. Chamberlain spoke in 1897. Six years afterwards we had to accept Lord Alverstone's views of our dispute with the United States, and (speaking, of course, merely for myself) I should much rather, without having had behind us the "great military and naval power of Great Britain," have acceded at once to the United States demands than, with a pretence of the possession of such power, have been compelled not only to suffer loss, but to attribute it to the weakness of a British government and the treachery of an English judge. And who would not rather have withdrawn our sealing-ships from the Pacific because the United States demanded it, than because the British navy helped the American cruisers to chase us from the open seas? Mr. Chamberlain's argument at the Conference had, quite naturally, no effect upon Canada. We were not haunted with fear of the United States. We knew that we might have disputes with our neighbors, but we knew pretty well what would become of them.

In 1902, Mr. Chamberlain was still more insistent. He had expended over $1,250,000,000 in the Boer war, and he upbraided us for not contributing more than we did. Again he reminded us of our danger, and presented a memorandum from the Admiralty, which contained the following very remarkable statement as to what our position would be if we had not the British navy behind us:—

"The Dominion of Canada would have to frame its naval policy with a view to the navy of the United States" (a).

We should, of course, do nothing of the kind, for our danger would be along the boundary line and not on the ocean. With the other colonies, Mr. Chamberlain's arguments had, for obvious reasons, very much more effect, and his efforts were rewarded with agreements to pay the following annual contributions:

Cape Colony	£ 50,000
Australia	200,000
New Zealand	40,000
Natal	35,000
Newfoundland	3,000

(a) Proceedings, p. 19.

For the next five years, Canada had to suffer contumely and insult because she was the only self-governing colony that declined to depart from her traditional line of national development, and to become a purchaser of defence. The next Conference (1907) brought her completest justification. By that time experience had worked the conversion not only of Australia, but of the British government, and the Admiralty itself. They all agreed that Canada was right. Mr. Deakin (Australia) said:

"Australia's responsibility (for naval defence) is now fixed on a monetary standard; and we submit that this is not the most acceptable standard for Australia, nor is it likely to further the objects that we have, or the objects that you have, in maintaining the present contribution" (a).

"In Australia, for reasons which have already been put on record in the despatch which I had the honor of addressing to the Admiralty about two years ago, *the existing contribution has not proved generally popular.* It was passed because it was felt that some distinct recognition of our responsibility for the defence of our own country, and of the Empire of which it is a part, was necessary, and though it did not take the form which commended itself most to the very large minority, possibly even a majority of the electors, we accepted that mode of co-operation until some better presented itself. *Further consideration has convinced the public that the present agreement is not satisfactory either to the Admiralty, the political or professional Lords of the Admiralty, or to the parliament of the Commonwealth*" (b).

Mr. Moore (Natal) said:

"But I do trust that the Admiralty will meet us in getting that contribution made more in the direction which I have tried to indicate than by simply *a cold lump sum, voted on our estimates, for which we have no actual evidence as directly concerning the people we represent*" (c).

General Botha (Transvaal) said:

"I think that at present we are so constituted in the Transvaal that we shall find it difficult to make a contribution to the navy by way of a money payment"(d).

Lord Tweedmouth (the First Lord) spoke of the advantage derivable from the change of plan:—

"You cannot take the small craft, such as torpedo boats and submarines, across the ocean; and for warships to arrive in South Africa, or in Australia or in New Zealand or in Canada, and find ready to hand well-trained men in good vessels of this kind would be an enormous advantage to them. It would be an enormous advantage to find ready to their hand, men well trained, ready to take

(a) Ibid, p. 132.
(b) Ibid, p. 473.
(c) Ibid, p. 146.
(d) Ibid, p. 147.

part in the work of the fleet. There is, I think, the further advantage in these small flotillas, that they will be *an admirable means of coast defence; that you will be able by the use of them to avoid practically all danger from any sudden raid which might be made by a cruising squadron"* (a).

All this speaks for itself and is, I think, conclusive upon the question whether we should send a cheque each year to the Admiralty or should construct ships of our own. I do not dwell upon the other considerations leading to the same conclusion—namely, those based upon the beneficial effect upon our national life and so on. They are sufficiently familiar. The argument which I present is the one based upon experience.

What Sort of a Navy?

If we are to have a navy, the only remaining question is as to its character. But that is a matter rather for the experts than for me. At the same time, I may be permitted to say that the considerations to which I have alluded seem to support the conclusion at which the Admiralty and our government have arrived.

I trust that what I have said may be of assistance in the formation of correct judgment upon this very important question. If I had any doubt as to the propriety of the course which we have adopted, it would be overwhelmed in my gratification at its splendid significance as an assertion of our nationhood. Nothing can more clearly and conspicuously evidence sovereignty than war-ships flying the flag of their country. By the direct order of our King, our navy is to be known as THE ROYAL CANADIAN NAVY. It is a Canadian navy. It is not a part of the British navy, although it may, when necessity arises, co-operate with the ships of the white ensign. Unless at any time otherwise ordered by ourselves it is to remain "exclusively under the control of Canada." And at the jack staff of every ship is to be flown "THE DISTINCTIVE FLAG OF THE DOMINION" (b).

Mr. Arthur J. Balfour.

Although not perfctly pertinent to the subject under discussion, I cannot refrain from reproducing a sentence recently spoken by Mr. Balfour:—

(a) Ibid. p. 131.
(b) Cd. 5746–2, p. I.

"I BELIEVE, FROM A LEGAL POINT OF VIEW, THE BRITISH PARLIAMENT IS SUPREME OVER THE PARLIAMENT OF CANADA OR AUSTRALASIA, OR THE CAPE, OR SOUTH AFRICA. BUT IN FACT, THEY ARE INDEPENDENT PARLIAMENTS, ABSOLUTELY INDEPENDENT —(cheers)—AND IT IS OUR BUSINESS TO RECOGNIZE THAT AND TO FRAME THE BRITISH EMPIRE UPON THE CO-OPERATION OF ABSOLUTELY INDEPENDENT PARLIAMENTS" (a).

In Canada we reserve our cheers, I am afraid, for anti-imperialism and anti-Americanism. We do not sufficiently realize that absolute independence is but the affirmative corollary of these negatives. In England (as I have before remarked) the position is much better understood; and, it is a splendid encouragement to Canadian nationalists that the generous cheers which followed Mr. Balfour's assertion of the parliamentary independence of Canada should have come from the country which waged war against the asserted independence of the other British-American colonies.

Upon another occasion Mr. Balfour said:—

"It is a matter of common knowledge—and, may I add, not a matter of regret, but *a matter of pride and rejoicing*—that the great Dominions beyond the seas are becoming great nations in themselves." (b).

Thank heaven, the voice of imperialistic disparagement of Canadian efficiency, and Canadian nationhood, is rapidly failing. Ere long there will not be a single Canadian who will refuse to join in his British brother's acclaim of that, which to every subject of the King, ought to be, and will be "A MATTER OF PRIDE AND REJOICING."

JOHN S. EWART.

Ottawa, December, 1911.

(a) *Times*, 1 Feb, 1911.
(b) House of Commons, 21 July, 1910.

CPSIA information can be obtained
at www.ICGtesting.com
Printed in the USA
BVHW09*1111160818
524721BV00018B/2505/P